ideals®
FRIENDSHIP

More Than 50 Years of Celebrating Life's Most Treasured Moments

Vol. 59, No. 4

Friend is a word of royal tone. Friend is a poem all alone.
—*Author Unknown*

IDEALS—Vol. 59, No. 4 July MMII IDEALS (ISSN 0019-137X, USPS 256-240)
is published six times a year: January, March, May, July, September, and November by
IDEALS PUBLICATIONS, a division of Guideposts
39 Seminary Hill Road, Carmel, NY 10512.
Copyright © MMII by IDEALS PUBLICATIONS, a division of Guideposts.
All rights reserved. The cover and entire contents of IDEALS are fully protected by copyright
and must not be reproduced in any manner whatsoever.
Title IDEALS registered U.S. Patent Office. Printed and bound in USA by Quebecor Printing.

Printed on Weyerhaeuser Husky. The paper used in this publication meets the minimum requirements of
American National Standard for Information Sciences—
Permanence of Paper for Printed Library Materials, ANSI Z39.48-1984.

Periodicals postage paid at Carmel, New York, and additional mailing offices.
POSTMASTER: Send address changes to Ideals, 39 Seminary Hill Road, Carmel, NY 10512.
For subscription or customer service questions, contact Ideals Publications,
a division of Guideposts, 39 Seminary Hill Road, Carmel, NY 10512. Fax 845-228-2115.

Reader Preference Service: We occasionally make our mailing lists available to
other companies whose products or services might interest you.
If you prefer not to be included, please write to Ideals Customer Service.

ISBN 0-8249-1202-0 GST 893989236

Visit the *Ideals* website at www.idealsbooks.com

*Cover Photo: Stargazer bouquet. Photo by Bruce Jackson/Gnass Photo Images.
Inside Front Cover:* MIRRORED LILIES. *Mary Kay Krell, artist.
Inside Back Cover:* AN IMPROMPTU BALL, 1899. *Eva Roos, artist. Image from Christie's.*

From Summer's Golden Casement

Louise Weibert Sutton

From summer's golden casement
I prize her August view:
Sunshine across the flowers;
Warm bees in rendezvous;
Broad butterflies, bright-winging
Skyward in airy grace;
While nature, now full-bosomed,
Rests with a smiling face.

From summer's golden casement
I hear blithe redbirds call;
Yet somehow, past the meadows,
I sense the coming fall.

And so I cherish deeper
These moments as they pass,
Knowing they, like grains of sand,
Soon trickle through the glass.

I cannot tell how winter
Will match my hopes or moods;
But now, content, I savor
These hours in gratitude.

I hope in memory's garden,
In duller waiting hours,
To find with joy, transplanted,
The summer's brightest flowers.

Summer Insured

Ethel S. Chappell

Against the cold, dark days of deepest winter,
I stored some precious hours plucked from May,
Preserved them with the fragrance of June roses
Pressed down with birdsong from a July day.

I garnered basketfuls of August sunshine
And sprinkled in the dust of myriad stars;
And round it all I tucked in summer's friendships,
Then placed them on the shelf like sweet rose jars.

When January winds howl down the chimney
And February snowflakes fill the air,
I open wide the doors to mem'ry's storehouse,
And summer's all around my fireside chair.

Summer wildflowers blend into a pastel field. Photo by A. Jackamets/H. Armstrong Roberts.

SWEET SUMMERTIME

William Howitt

Who has not dreamed a world of bliss
On a bright, sunny noon like this,
Couched by his native brook's green maze
With comrade of his boyish days
While all around them seemed to be
Just as in joyous infancy?
Who has not loved at such an hour,
Upon that heath in birchen bower,
Lulled in the poet's dreamy mood,
Its wild and sunny solitude?
While o'er the waste of purple ling,
You make a sultry glimmering;
Silence herself there seems to sleep,
Wrapped in a slumber long and deep.
Where slowly stray those lonely sheep
Through the tall foxglove's crimson bloom,
And gleaming of the scattered broom,
Love you not, then to list and hear
The crackling of the gorse flowers near,
Pouring an orange-scented tide
Of fragrance o'er the desert wide?
To hear the buzzard's whimpering shrill,
Hovering above you high and still?
The twittering of the bird that dwells
Among the heath's delicious bells?
While round your bed, o'er fern and blade,
Insects in green and gold arrayed,
The sun's gay tribes have lightly strayed
And sweeter sound their humming wings
Than the proud minstrel's echoing strings.

Right: Pink monkey-flower climbs among the rocks along the
Paradise River in Mount Rainier National Park, Washington.
Photo by Terry Donnelly.
Overleaf: Sunflowers create their own
hill of gold near Weiser, Idaho.
Photo by Carr Clifton.

Shades of Blue

Angie Davidson Bass

Hydrangeas bloomed along the way
Beside an old rock wall today;
And as I drank deep of beauty rare,
A bluebird flashed its wings so fair.

Then came a child with bluest eyes
That matched the blue of summer skies
And brought to me a sweet bouquet
Of larkspur blooming by the way.

Then swirling mists of indigo
Adorned the shimmering hills below

And raced to meet the sapphire light
That prophesied the coming night.

Shades of blue were my delight
Throughout the day and into night
As campfires gleamed with blue rings curled
In moonlight round a blue-tinged world.

And wild blue asters fringed the lane
That brought me, singing, home again.

Blue Is a Bit of Heaven

Juanita Johnson

I find a bit of heaven
In the blue of a baby's eyes,
In the blue of spreading feathers
As a bluebird soars the skies,
In the blue of morning glories
Clinging where old fences run,

In the blue of silent waters
When the day is almost done.
Yes, I find a bit of heaven
In this soft and tranquil hue;
God created for our pleasure
Many, many things of blue.

*Blue oakleaf hydrangeas line a path in Manteo, North Carolina,
with a bit of heaven. Photo by Mary Liz Austin.*

Readers' Reflections

Editor's Note: Readers are invited to submit original poetry for possible publication in future issues of Ideals. Please send typed copies only; manuscripts will not be returned. Writers receive $10 for each published submission. Send material to Readers' Reflections, Ideals Publications, 535 Metroplex Drive, Suite 250, Nashville, Tennessee 37211.

Early August Morning

Evalyn Torrant
Midland, Michigan

The sky's a shell of pink and oyster.
Beneath green leaves the path's a cloister.
Like shadows on the quiet stream
Two mallards raise gold bills to preen
While white upon the grassy swells
Of the empty park moor fleets of gulls.
Each bloom with dewy spangles glows;
Soft drifts the fragrance of the rose.

Friends

C. David Hay
Rosedale, Indiana

To offer trust in times of need,
To see misfortune through,
To feel the pain when you are cut
Because they bleed some too.

To make no judgment heedlessly,
To defend from idle talk,
To know that only you can wear
The shoes in which you walk.

To share a tear in sadness,
To be first with a hand,
To be forgiving of mistakes
Because they understand.

Grace and glory fade with time;
No one can stem the flow.
Treasured be life's bondings
That never cease to grow.

There is no greater tribute
To which one can ascend
Than to earn the simple title—
The one that's called a friend.

Summer's End

Anita Phillips
Westborough, Massachusetts

These are the precious moments
I wait for all summer long,
When the last flower withers,
Heat and humidity finally gone.
When milky skies are wiped away,
Replaced by purest azure blue,
Each dawn will break with golden sun
Crystal clear as morning dew.

Silver shines on blackest velvet.
Gone are murky evening skies;
Stars show brightly there once more
Like millions of angelic eyes.
The moon hangs low in naked grace,
Bereft of clouds and summer haze—
How well defined its old man's face!

The first few streaks of autumn color
Burning through the summer green
Lift my spirits as none other;
For autumn soon will reign supreme.

Holding On

Myrle Glace
Upper Holland, Pennsylvania

Things I hold on to,
Cannot seem to part with:
Old slippers, old robes,
Old pictures and books,
Old jeans and sweatshirts.
I guess you get the idea.
It's hard for me to let go;
I get attached.

Imagine then how much more
I treasure and hold on to you,
My beloved friend.
I think of you, miss you,
And wonder with concern
About your health, your life,
And when, if ever, I'll see you again.

A Friend Is That Someone

Gene Scott
Livonia, Michigan

Someone to talk with,
No notice required.
Someone to walk with
When that is desired.
Someone to be with
And so glad to share.
Someone to help with
A fret or a care.

Someone to laugh with
Over simple delights.
Someone to roam with
And see all the sights.
Someone to sigh with
Or enjoy a surprise.
Someone to cry with
When troubles arise.

A friend is that someone,
So steady and true,
The one who will always
Be there for you.
A friend is that someone
On whom you rely,
Who comes to your aid
With no questions why.

Remember When

SUMMER GARDEN

Marjorie Holmes

Each day we were learning a lesson that no child of the supermarket can appreciate: that Nature, for all her bounty, gives you nothing scot-free. Soon we were being ordered forth with hoes merely to keep the weeds at bay. Or to chase off the rabbits, merry little hide-and-seek enemies that you couldn't hate even when they neatly sheared off an entire row of your very best broccoli. And though we fretted and fussed about aching backs and blisters, and ran in to look at the clock ticking away on the kitchen table, and begged to join the friends who'd managed their own release—the garden was a hot, humming, secretive, pungently sweet, and tantalizing place. Its many products were somehow like little people manifesting their different personalities.

The peas had an air of precious superiority. Their tendrils wound gracefully up the props and clung with delicate fingers; their blossoms were like tiny, white bows in their hair. So few were they at first that you cheated, picking some that were barely formed. But peas develop fast. Soon their abundance made their gathering urgent. "Hurry, go pick the peas, or they'll be too old."

The pods became long and fat, so full some were bursting. No need to steal the flat ones, or those whose tough yellowing hides informed you you were already too late. Like people who have too swiftly reached their prime, they had had their change, poor things.

The vessels overflowed. Sitting on sunny back steps, you shelled them. Birds sang, mothers worked in kitchens, screen doors banged. There was the crisp snapping of the pods. With a sensation vaguely sensuous, your fingers rooted out the emeralds they contained. Some you ate raw—juicy, flat, and definitely sweet. The shells piled up on a newspaper like the wreckage of mighty fleets. You saved a few for little boats and sailed them later across a puddle or a big tin tub.

Potatoes were a lustier vegetable, but when they were babies they were creamed with peas to form a dish that would make the gods throw away their ambrosia and abandon Parnassus for our backyard.

Potato vines (like tomatoes) have starry blossoms, and potatoes are fun to dig. Grandpa always used a pitchfork, since the blade of spade or hoe was likely to slice them in two. I can see him yet, tall and handsome and white-moustached, the clods raining softly through his lifted tines, a few potatoes clinging to the root like small brown gnomes. The rest were buried treasure scattered about, and you hunted them with almost the same anticipation as you hunted eggs. These first little new potatoes had skin so fragile it could be scrubbed off with a stiff brush. The flesh underneath was rosy, exactly like that of children whose mother had washed their faces too hard.

Beans were pleasant to pick. They hung like lumpy pendants in the bushy forests of their growth, slender, green string beans or the yellow wax ones that had a tallowy luster like their name. Surrounded by cohorts, you were set to snapping and "stringing" them for the pot, already fragrant with ham or bacon, bubbling on the range. There is nothing more delicious than fresh-cooked beans, and time only enhances their flavor when they're cold. Often, snooping in the icebox at bedtime, there would be a squabble over how to scoop aside the grease and finish off a bowl.

Sweet corn was royal fare. It grew tall and stately out by the alley, hobnobbing with the hollyhocks and sunflowers. On hot nights you could sometimes hear it crackling as it stretched its joints toward the stars, like the field corn on nearby farms. We

A young green-thumb returns from the garden with the day's bounty. Photo by H. Armstrong Roberts.

watched its development with hungry eyes, measuring our own growth against it, standing on tiptoe sometimes to pull aside the rosy sills and test the kernels with a fingernail. When the ears were ready, they spurted milk, and off you streaked with the news. In a blissful suspense, you waited while Father or Grandfather came to check; and what joy when he broke the ear free, stripped the husks aside and waved the nude ear aloft like some triumphant offering. "Sweet corn for supper!" The word spread. And we came squealing like pigs to the trough and ate it from the steaming golden platters with butter dripping down our chins.

But nothing could surpass a tomato picked and eaten, still sun hot, on a drowsy summer's afternoon. And no fragrance is more pungent than that of tomato vines when you brush against them in the

dewy dusk playing Hide-and-Go-Seek or Run, Sheep, Run. The branches were bowed with the scarlet globes; and when they could bear no more, you gathered them into bushel baskets and lugged them into the kitchen. . . .

I dream sometimes of those abundant summers in memory's lost emerald land of Oz. I wish my children could make little boats out of new-picked pods, and eat green apples, and raid a watermelon patch. I wish they could wake up some morning and find a scarecrow grinning at them from a bird-ringing cherry tree.

Since they can't, I want them to know that fruits and vegetables don't grow on the shelves of a supermarket, to be had solely for money and the opening of packages. Somewhere they are being born and harvested by human hands out of God's own earth and sky and sun and rain.

Little Paths

Grace V. Watkins

I love a little path that winds
Along beside a stream
With flowers bordering it more sweet,
More fair than any dream.

I love a little path that leads
To a little country church
Where prayers are said more beautifully
Than wind through groves of birch.

I love a little path that brings
Me home from far away
To a kitchen where fresh cookies wait
At any time of day.

But most, I love a little path
From my heart into yours
That we can travel any time,
Then softly close the doors
And know the warm companionship,
The sweetness never old,
More bright and fair than any rose,
Than any shining gold.

A flagstone path offers a colorful view of the garden.
Photo by Jessie Walker.

From My Garden Journal

Lisa Ragan

CANNA

I harbor a long-held dream of someday living in a pastel-colored Victorian home complete with gingerbread details and lush gardens. In my imagination, the gardens surrounding my home feature well-tended, blossoming plants in pale colors. I redesign this fantasy garden as I learn of flowers that were popular during the Victorian era. For example, when I heard that Victorian gardeners doted on cannas, I placed a row of stately, redheaded cannas along the back fence. But the bright red blaze of their blooms seemed out of place in my pastel fairytale. Happily, I learned that modern-day gardeners can grow cannas in a variety of colors, including several pastel shades. I've since revised the cannas in my dream garden to a variety that produces apricot-colored blossoms—a perfect solution to my imaginary dilemma.

The canna grows perennially in the tropics and can be grown as an annual throughout most of the United States. An exotic-looking plant that ranges in heights from one-and-a-half feet to nine feet, the canna features broad, oval leaves in solid or variegated colors ranging from muddy burgundy to bronze to deep green. The leaves themselves can grow between two and three feet long and spiral up the canna's sturdy stalk. At the top, clusters of vivid blooms stretch skyward in colors that range from bright red, orange, fuchsia, and yellow to softer shades of apricot, blush, and creamy white.

Cannas grew throughout the southern United States long before the Victorians fell in love with them. Native to Central and South America and the Pacific tropics, the canna was first documented in the United States in 1777 by botanist William Bartram. While traveling in the South, Bartram came upon *Canna indica* growing in the wetlands of southern Louisiana. This species of canna grows about five feet and features reddish stems, large leaves tinged with bronze, and striking crimson flowers.

The canna's common name, Indian shot, originally applied specifically to *Canna indica* but now refers to the canna in general. The name *Indian shot* comes from the legend that South Americans Indians once used the strong, pea-sized seeds of the canna plant as ammunition. The popularity of canna plants has grown steadily through the years; and by the time of the Victorians, cannas could be found throughout the United States and Europe.

Most cannas today can be found under the label *Canna x generalis*, a name that aptly fits the canna's heritage of intermingled species. Cannas have been hybridized extensively; and with so many flower colors, height options, and leaf vari-

CANNA

eties, the cannas of today barely resemble the cannas of our Victorian ancestors. But some of the old favorites are still available, such as Red King Humbert (also known as Le Roi Humbert), a tall variety that can grow up to nine feet and offers traditional scarlet blossoms and reddish leaves touched with bronze. A dwarf variety that reaches only three feet, President reigns as another of the old-fashioned favorites and produces red flowers and glossy green leaves. In pastel-blossomed varieties, gardeners can choose from Garbo (a dwarf cultivar with salmon pink flowers and ruby-colored leaves), Richard Wallace (a canna of medium height with buttery yellow blossoms and apple green leaves), or Apricot Ice (a dwarf canna with soft, yellowish-orange flowers and green leaves). For striking foliage, Tropicanna produces large leaves striped with yellow, orange, maroon, and lime green. Weekend gardeners particularly love Pink Futurity, but not just for its lovely pink flowers and attractive foliage edged in maroon. Pink Futurity grooms itself by dropping its own blossoms when past their prime.

Cannas are tuberous plants that grow from a root-like rhizome instead of a bulb. After the last spring frost, rhizomes should be planted two to three inches deep and one foot to two feet apart (depending on height at maturity) in fertile, slightly damp soil that receives full sun. Once established, water thoroughly once a week. Young canna plants can also be planted in a similar fashion after the last frost. Cannas bloom from mid to late summer until the first autumn frost. Remove dead flower heads and seedpods throughout the blooming season to encourage new blossoms. Because of its rapid growth and profuse blooming, cannas benefit from regular applications of a balanced fertilizer. Also, a light mulch will help the plants retain moisture. Despite the impressive heights that many varieties can attain, cannas do not need staking. Their thick stalks act as veritable fence posts and hold up the immense leaves and brilliant flowers on their own.

The canna thrives in hot, humid climates and can survive as a perennial in the warmest regions of the United States. For the rest of the country, gardeners must dig up canna rhizomes after fall frost has blackened the leaves and stems. Carefully shake excess dirt off the rhizomes, cover with dampened peat, and store them in a cool, dark place (ideally between 40 and 50 degrees Fahrenheit). Check the peat periodically throughout the winter to ensure continued dampness. The rhizomes can be replanted in the spring after the last frost. Spring is also the best time to divide cannas for propagation. Some brave gardeners in climates with moderate winters overwinter their cannas by planting them in protected areas and providing them with a thick covering of mulch, straw, and leaves.

With such a tropical appearance, cannas work best as background plants or when planted as a small group to add a splash of color. They are particularly striking when planted en masse and make pleasing living fences. Since the canna can be grown successfully in a large pot, city gardeners can add color to the patio by adding a single canna.

Resistant to most diseases, cannas can be bothered by a few pests. Strips of copper placed around canna seedlings will repel hungry snails and slugs. In the Southern states, gardeners should be on the lookout for the larger and lesser leaf roller on their canna plants. Contact a local nursery for advice on how to eliminate them once they are discovered.

Although the imaginary garden surrounding my Victorian dream home changes often, the stately row of cannas along the back fence remains and now includes every pastel shade. I know I'll continue to design cannas into the gardens of my daydreams, and perhaps some day I may even find a place to plant some real-life cannas in my real-life backyard.

A Prayer at Summer's End

(A FARM WIFE'S LITANY)

Ruby Jones

For fruit warm ripe in summer's sun,
For love and work and wholesome fun,
For raindrops on the windowpanes,
For walks down grassy country lanes,
For sunshine bright, for moonlight's glow,
For cornstalks marching row on row,
For baby pigs, for laughter gay,
For fragrant smell of new-mown hay,
For food and music, birdsongs sweet,
For restful, healing nighttime sleep,
For home with its familiar joys,
For carefree shouts of girls and boys,
For safe returns, for loving care,
For all the bliss of answered prayer,
For dancing stars, for firelight's gleam,
Fulfillment of a cherished dream,
For books and friends, a faith that sings,
For happiness homecoming brings,
For hope renewed, for courage born,
For breathless hush of early morn,
For this—a blessed interlude—
Dear God, accept my gratitude.

A quaint front porch offers views of summer's last days.
Photo by Stefan Lawrence/ImageState.

GENERATIONS

On a recent bright, late-summer afternoon, I attended a party at the home of my friends Nancy and Joe. The lake was shimmering, the skies were clear blue, and the flowers at the edge of the water brought the gold and purple hues of autumn to the spacious lawn. It was as if all of nature knew we were celebrating something special. The party was in honor of eight-week-old Justin, the nephew of Nancy and Joe. After a difficult stay in the hospital, newborn Justin had finally returned home.

As a friend of the family, I was invited to the party, and I had the honor of holding the baby in my arms. Here I was, in my ninety-second year up the long hill of life; and in my arms was tiny Justin, with many generations separating us. I talked to him about my love for nature, my friendship with the hills. He looked directly at me, seemingly taking in each word as I spoke of the wonders of the seasons and told him of the animals, trees, and valleys he would one day discover.

It has been many years since I was a young farmboy learning the ways of nature; yet I remember those days happily and wish as many adventures and rich experiences for Justin. I wonder if his early steps will lead him toward the fields and into the hills as mine did. As this small member of the next generation leaves his footprints on the new century, I will eagerly watch to see where the bridges of life lead him.

The author of three books, Lansing Christman has contributed to Ideals *for almost thirty years. Mr. Christman has also been published in several American, international, and braille anthologies. He lives in rural South Carolina.*

*A covered bridge spans the Clearfork-Mohican River in Ohio's Mohican State Park.
Photo by Terry Donnelly.*

Passing

Louise Moss Montgomery

There is a bluish-purple haze
That hangs upon the heavy grasses,
A prophecy of autumn days
    As summer passes.

There is a burst of brilliant bloom
Within the gated garden closes,
A silent spilling of perfume
    From autumn roses.

There is a heated, hectic hue
Upon the face of fruit and flower
As waning summer flames anew
    Its final hour.

Vermilion and topaz tints
Upon the lovely leaves are showing,
And everything in nature hints
    The summer's going.

Passing By

Grace Cornell Tall

What great hero passes now
Triumphant through our town
That trees wear gold
And wave and bow
And fling confetti down?

It must be some celebrity;
And yet, I wonder why
These miles around I only see
Summer passing by.

The family cat takes his leisure while awaiting the next croquet game. Photo by Jessie Walker.

The Jar of Jelly

Barbara Overton Christie

To others' eyes, it may not look like much;
"It's just a jar of jelly," some would say,
"Wrapped up in festive ribbons and some seals
To make it look more festive and more gay."
But you for whom it's meant will find, I know,
All that is packed within the little jar.
You will translate the label properly
And see just what the contents really are.
"Wild grape," you'll say, and suddenly
You'll not be walking dusty city halls

But down an autumn-gilded, little lane
Between the jewelled vines of old stone walls.
Instead of dingy bricks beyond a court,
You'll see a spruce-green hillside, sharp and clear.
Sweet fern and bayberry will scent the breeze;
The whirr of partridge wings delight your ear.
It is not much to send, this one small jar;
But you will see that in it, pure and true,
Shimmers the essence of the place we love,
Preserved especially by me, for you.

Jewels

Emily Buzby

I know a way of catching summer
　　sunbeams as they play
And, like a crafty alchemist of old,
Of turning them to gems and molten gold
For winter when the skies are dull and gray.

In crystal jars upon my shelf they stand:
The ruby juice of currants and the bland,
Cool amber of the peach, the sapphire blue
Of wild grapes and of damsons wet with dew,
The coral of the quince, the pearly sheen
Of silver pears, the mint leaf's emerald green.

Strung on a chain of golden summer hours,
Clasped with the drone of bees
　　and scent of flowers.
Row upon row my captured sunbeams stand
Like jewels of India or gems from Samarkand.

Heavy clusters of ripe grapes dangle from the vines in Napa Valley, California. Photo by D. Carriere/H. Armstrong Roberts.

Ideals' Family Recipes

As young children, we learn that almost any food, from macaroni to broccoli, tastes better with cheese on it. Here we offer five more ways to enjoy this lifelong favorite. We would love to try your favorite family recipe too. Send a typed copy to Ideals Publications, 535 Metroplex Drive, Suite 250, Nashville, TN 37211. We pay $10 for each recipe published.

Cordon Bleu Casserole
Helen L. Musenbrock of O'Fallon, Missouri

2 cups frozen mixed vegetables	1 cup julienned cooked ham
1 10½-ounce can cream-of-mushroom soup, divided	½ cup grated Swiss cheese
1½ cups julienned cooked chicken	4 ounces dry stuffing mix
	4 tablespoons melted butter

Preheat oven to 350° F. In a lightly greased 2-quart casserole, layer frozen mixed vegetables, half of the soup, chicken, remaining soup, ham, cheese, and stuffing mix. Pour melted butter over top. Cover tightly with foil and bake 45 minutes. Serve hot. Makes 8 servings.

Family Favorite Green Beans
Mildred Burns of Chattanooga, Tennessee

3 tablespoons butter	¼ teaspoon salt
1 medium onion, cut into eighths	⅛ teaspoon pepper
1 10-ounce package frozen French-style green beans	8 ounces fresh mushrooms, cut into thirds
½ teaspoon rosemary	½ cup shredded Monterey Jack cheese

In large saucepan, melt butter. Stir in onion; cook over medium heat 2 to 3 minutes or until tender. Add beans, rosemary, salt, and pepper. Cover; continue cooking, stirring occasionally, 3 to 5 minutes or until beans are thawed and separated. Remove cover. Stir in mushrooms; continue cooking until beans are crisply tender. Sprinkle with cheese. Cover; let stand 1 minute. Makes 4 servings.

Cauliflower au Gratin

Naomi Dyer of Eaton, Colorado

1   clove garlic, minced
½   cup chopped, cooked ham
6   tablespoons butter
1   head cauliflower, broken into florets
1½ cups heavy cream
2   tablespoons all-purpose flour

¼   teaspoon salt
    Pepper to taste
⅛   teaspoon cayenne pepper
1½ cups shredded Swiss cheese
3   tablespoons chopped, fresh parsley

Preheat oven broiler. In a large skillet, sauté garlic and ham in butter over medium heat for 2 minutes. Add cauliflower; stir and cook until tender but still crisp. In a small bowl, combine cream, flour, salt, pepper, and cayenne pepper. Blend well with whisk. Slowly stir flour mixture into skillet. Cook and stir until thickened; simmer 1 additional minute. Pour into a 2-quart baking dish. Sprinkle with cheese. Place under broiler until lightly browned, about 2 to 4 minutes. Sprinkle with parsley and serve immediately. Makes 8 servings.

Cheesy Potatoes

Phyllis M. Peters of Three Rivers, Michigan

2   pounds frozen hash-browned potatoes
1   10½-ounce cream-of-chicken soup
½   cup sour cream

1   tablespoon dried onion flakes
½   cup butter, sliced
1   cup shredded Cheddar cheese

Preheat oven to 350° F. Allow potatoes to partially thaw. In a large mixing bowl, combine potatoes with remaining ingredients. Mix well, then spread in lightly buttered 13-by-9-by-2-inch baking dish. Bake 90 minutes; serve hot. Makes 8 servings.

Macadamia Cheese Hors d'Oeuvres

Margaret Anderson of Dunkerton, Iowa

¼   cup butter, softened
1   cup biscuit mix
1   egg, slightly beaten

1   cup chopped macadamia nuts
½   cup shredded Cheddar cheese
    Cayenne pepper to taste

Preheat oven to 400° F. In a large bowl, cut butter into biscuit mix until coarse crumbs form. Stir in egg, nuts, cheese, and pepper. Mix well. Drop by teaspoons onto lightly greased cookie sheet. Bake 8 minutes. Makes 48 pieces.

Friendship

Anne Campbell

Since you have broken bread with me,
Home has an added quality.
I loved its coziness before,
The sunlight on the velvet floor,
The few old treasures I so prize,
The toys strewn through it, children-wise,
The clock that ticked me up the stairs
To Mother's arms and childish prayers.

But when you found my door at last
And through its wide-flung portals passed,
You brought with you a radiance
That stayed when you departed hence.
Staunch love and true has ever graced
Our dwelling and its rafters braced;
And friendship's lingered joyously
Since you have broken bread with me.

We Have Broken
Our Bread Together

Edwin Markham

We have broken our bread together, and now we part.
We have broken the bread of the mind and the bread of the heart.
We may never meet again till another star,
But we shall be friends together wherever we are.

This is no time for lamenting, no moment for sighs.
Let us trust and be glad, see the truth in each other's eyes.
Let us smile as we wave farewell where the long road bends.
Let us sing to the vow that makes us forever friends.

A laden antique plate rack overlooks a table set for tea. Photo by Jessie Walker.

Child-Wise

Margie Holliday

We spoke of bread and simple things
Like cellared fruit and crocks of cream.
Our thoughts sailed forth on rising wings
And flew far back to reach the gleam
Of former years. We talked of youth
In tones of joy, and every voice
Recalled with warmth a childhood truth.
We thought again of that early choice
Of cool, sweet milk and a slice of bread,
And how, as children, we beamed our praise
As eager mouths were amply fed.
Hunger grew strong on autumn days;
How good the taste of crust and crumb.
The food was plain, but savored through,
Whether we chose a pear or plum.
Oh, then the world was fresh with glow;
Each moment held innate delight.
We gazed ahead with trusting eyes,
With never a thought of want or fright.
Oh, to be a child again, and wise.

Norwegian painting techniques decorate door and wall in this quaint kitchen.
Photo by Jessie Walker.

THROUGH MY WINDOW

— Pamela Kennedy —

Art by Meredith Johnson

LET'S PRETEND

When I was a little girl, I loved to play pretend. Mother would pass along her old clothes to my dress-up box. Then when my best friend, Susan, came over, we'd deck ourselves in crepe and rayon, arrange our cloche hats, wrap ourselves in fox or beaver, and clomp up the street in our oversized pumps. So convincing was our disguise that on one occasion a neighbor called my mother to report that two female dwarfs had just walked past her house! It's been over five decades since those days, but I've recently connected with a whole new group of friends who allow me to periodically return to this favorite youthful pastime.

I found these new friends quite by accident one day while doing research for a church program. I wanted to put together a series of readings from the journals of the New England Congregationalist missionaries who had first arrived in the Hawaiian Islands in the 1820s. The logical place to begin was the Mission Houses Museum in Honolulu. What I discovered there was much more than dry, dusty journals. I found a group of people who were dedicated to bringing history to life by dressing up and playing pretend.

The leader of this band of pretenders is a vivacious woman named Honey. Adept at not only crafting a script from the writings of the missionaries, she can also convince the most reluctant actor that he or she actually has just endured several months on a sailing vessel coming around Cape Horn and is now earnestly dedicated to the education and salvation of the local residents of the Sandwich Islands!

Her partner in this endeavor is Tory, a talented clothing designer. Tory has produced an entire room-sized wardrobe closet filled with petticoats, dresses, caps, bonnets, suits, shirts, waistcoats, trousers, cravats, and other necessities—all created with excruciating attention to historical detail. Tory's closet is a pretender's dream come true.

And just what kinds of grown-ups like to play pretend? Well, we're really an eclectic group. Samuel is in his eighties (he refuses to add the second digit) and has adopted the persona of an English sea captain. Dressed in his nineteenth-century nautical togs, he is no longer just an ex-retailer and resident of a local retirement community. As a seasoned mariner, he visits the residents of the compound discussing bills of lading and the recent prices for goods imported on his vessels. Samuel isn't a one-dimensional character, however. He has also revealed a penchant for grog, the missionary ladies, and an occasional salty story.

Ruth, Barbara, and Sandy tie on their bonnets, don their printed frocks over yards of pin-tucked cotton petticoats, and forget their day jobs as nurse, accountant, and librarian. Sitting on the lawn in the leafy shadows of the breadfruit tree, they carefully appliqué and stitch together a quilt while contemplating the best way to deal with the increasing demands of the Hawaiian queen, Kaahumanu.

In the kitchen, Betty, a speech pathologist, ties on her full-length apron and teaches her daughters how to prepare a fish stew in an iron pot over the fire, then to bake bread in the adjacent brick oven. The girls—who would normally be cruising the shopping mall or playing video games—are barefooted in simple cotton smocks as they dutifully haul water from the hand pump in heavy wooden buckets.

When Edward, a local Episcopal priest, buttons on the black suit and white cravat of the mission doctor, his whole demeanor changes. He's no longer worried about hymns and homilies. He has a measles outbreak to contend with and a sailor in the upstairs bedroom delirious from a tropical fever. Then he has to check on a patient complaining of a toothache and make sure that the latest shipment of medicinal spirits is still safe in the underground storeroom below the frame house.

In the print shop, Harold, a former engineer, sweats in his leather apron over the hand-operated printing press, turning out copies of the Ten Commandments and the first gospel translated into Hawaiian. He peels the still-damp pages off the press and hands them to open-mouthed school children, captivated by his stories of how the missionaries and Hawaiians first learned about one another's languages.

And me? I'm sitting on a straight-backed chair in the parlor, dressed in a long-sleeved, blue empire waist frock with a white cotton "modesty" tucked demurely into the scooped neck. I have a white cap over my carefully parted hair and an old, leather-bound Bible on my lap. Today, I can forget about teaching high school. I'm having a conversation with a Hawaiian *kumu* (teacher) about the correct translation of a passage from the Gospel of John. Later we'll sing some hymns in Hawaiian and English and perhaps share a cup of tea.

As we go about our assigned roles, we try to remain in character while responding to one another and to those who visit us. Schoolchildren, tourists, and local residents wander through the museum grounds and houses, all the while watching, listening, and asking questions. We like to legitimize the time we spend giving tours and answering inquiries as providing a living history experience. But somehow I suspect that's not the only reason we're here. Deep down inside I think we're all relishing the opportunity to be as we once were—children dressed in hand-me-down clothes, spending time with our friends and playing "let's pretend."

Pamela Kennedy is a freelance writer of short stories, articles, essays, and children's books. Wife of a retired naval officer and mother of three children, she has made her home on both U.S. coasts and currently resides in Honolulu, Hawaii.

Bits *and* Pieces

People who cannot find time for recreation are obliged sooner or later to find time for illness.

—*John Wanamaker*

The real character of a man is found out by his amusements.

—*Sir Joshua Reynolds*

For when the One Great Scorer comes to write against your name,
He marks not that you won or lost, but how you played the game.

—*Grantland Rice*

We play the game; God keeps the score.

—*Erwin W. Lutzer*

*I*t is when a man ceases to do the things he has to do and does the things he likes to do that the character is revealed.

—*Lin Yü-t'ang*

A clear fire, a clean hearth, and the rigour of the game.

—*Charles Lamb*

*T*o set the cause above renown, to love the game above the prize.

—*Sir Henry John Newbolt*

*W*ork and play are an artificial pair of opposites because the best kind of play contains an element of work, and the most productive kind of work must include something of the spirit of play.

—*Sydney J. Harris*

*E*ach man appears for a little while to laugh and weep, to work and play.

—*A. W. Tozer*

Fisherman's Daughter

Gertrude Ryder Bennett

She liked to skip along the water's edge,
To gather shells and strangely treasured things,
To smell the ocean, hear along the sedge
The chanteys of the breeze. The lazy wings
Of gulls delighted her. She always found
Those tragic places where the falling tide
Had caught a minnow. She would watch the ground
For fiddler crabs to come with cautious stride
And shuffle out across their settlement
Of tiny holes, and she would laugh to see
Them scamper back again. And so she spent
The hours in simple, summer revelry.
A mermaid, caught in nets and brought ashore,
Would not have known as much of ocean lore.

Children are we
Of the restless sea,
Swelling in anger or sparkling in glee.
We follow and race
In shifting chase
Over boundless ocean space.

—BAYARD TAYLOR

*Lake Michigan batters the bulkheads around Point Betsie Lighthouse near
Frankfort, Michigan. Photo by Ken Dequaine.*

A SLICE OF LIFE

Douglas Malloch

Art by Eve DeGrie

THIS MUCH I NEED

This much I need and little more:
A sturdy tree beside my door
To teach me fortitude through all
The winds that rise, the snows that fall;
And then, whatever else man hath,
A lovely rose beside the path
To teach me beauty when the sweat
Of life would make my mind forget.

This much I need, whatever gear
I ask God for: a comrade near
To teach me love, a friend to sit
And talk of books a little bit
And speak of folks with kindly word
And tell the good things we have heard.
Ah, yes, this also God must send,
The quiet comfort of a friend.

This much I need, though so much more
I crave, I seek, I hunger for.
Whatever else I may desire,
I need a house, I need a fire,
A lovely rose, a sturdy tree,
And someone close to comfort me.
A bit to eat, a book to read—
Though much I ask, this much I need.

NEIGHBORS

Will Evans

The folk who till the soil and take their bread
From hillside earth have common griefs and joys;
They help in life and join to lay their dead
Away upon the hill. They teach their boys
And girls the need to share the seasons' toil
And teach them that the common pleasures grow,
When they are shared, like corn on fertile soil.
This is the life I've lived; these things I know.
I like to think, when I lie down at night,
That there are good neighbors across each hill,
Neighbors who gladly help me by daylight
And who, by night, will come to aid me still.
This is a lovely thought to have when day
Is done and threads of toil are laid away.

I find it thrilling to climb up a hill
And look down on the chimney smokes around.
It seems that I can never get my fill
Of such a picture etched against the ground.
These houses are all close enough to blend
Their thinned-out chimney smoke like lovers' breath
And whisper in smoke words, as friend to friend,
That such communion knows not mortal death.
I like to look down on my neighbors' fields—
On straight, clean rows of corn and shocks of wheat
That hug the ground like spots of light and yield
A harvest to the eyes that is rich meat.
O God of Earth, what sweeter blessing can
You give than goodly neighbors unto man?

Artist Linda Nelson Stocks captures a small-town summer day in SUMMER PASTURES.

In Tune

Florence Steigerwalt

I don't remember when I first began
To call you friend. One day I only know
The vague companionship that I'd seen grow
So imperceptibly turned gold and ran
In tune with all I'd thought or dared to plan.
Since then, you've been to me like music, low
Yet clear; a fire that throws its warm, bright glow
On me as on each woman, child, and man
And common things that lie within its rays.
You've been like wholesome food that stays the cry
Of hungry, groping minds. And like a star—
A self-sufficient star—you make me raise
My utmost being to a higher sky,
In tune, like you, with earth, yet wide and far.

Two friends study the tides in On the Beach *by Hermann Seeger.*
Image from Christie's.

COLLECTOR'S

In the early 1920s when Grandmama Louise was little, she didn't own a radio. Entertainment came in the form of books and story-telling. News came by news-paper; and by the time it reached her house, it was hardly breaking news. Radios had only recently been invented and were beginning to catch on in the cities, but such innovations were hard to come by on the dusty plains of Texas.

At last, Grandmama's older sister, Evelyn, purchased a radio when she graduated from college and brought it home to the family as a gift. Grandmama still has that radio, a tombstone-shaped, wooden box in good-but-scratchy working order. It's perched on top of her television, just keeping warm and collecting dust. But Grandmama says she remembers a time when her father hung on its every word.

Grandmama's radio is a tiny thing, not a big one like the types that used to be spotlighted in magazines. Her daddy, Early, was a tall, lanky man, so I can just picture him crouched closely next to it so as not to miss a single news brief or advertisement. In the afternoon, Louise, Evelyn, their brother Ralph, and their younger sister, Elaine, would edge him out so they could follow whatever enchanting soap drama was unfolding.

It was Grandmama's father who took radios to heart, for Early began to politely bide his time until he could afford another radio, one just for himself.

Early's radio collection began innocently enough. He first bought an RCA Radiola Senior. Its speaker had an S-shaped neck style with a wide megaphone opening that belted music and news bulletins throughout the entire house. But that was no reason not to invest in an RCA Radiola Jr. as well, which Early did shortly thereafter.

His guard must have been down when the Sears and Roebuck catalog arrived. Within its pages, he fell in love with a Thorola and paid over sixty dollars to make it his own. He loved how its elaborate tuning dials shone brightly from the fireplace mantle.

A radio was needed for his desk as well, since it was imperative that he be aware of every latest news development. A preacher, after all, must remain in the world but not of the world. Fittingly, he purchased a cathedral-style radio with which he could follow the presidential election while simultaneously drafting next Sunday morning's sermon.

For the living room, Early scouted out a Silvertone Five-Tube Receiver, reassuring his wife that it was a striking value, even though he had to pay twelve dollars down and eight dollars each month thereafter. With a console receiver and built-in reproducer, it was poised in a showy cabinet of dark mahogany with neat two-tone trim. The family all quickly gathered around it to catch the latest details surrounding the Hindenburg crash.

Eventually, he could not be without a radio at any time. He outfitted the stable with an inexpensive, plastic tabletop model. While filling the troughs with sweet feed, he'd be listening to stock quotes, commodity prices, and weather reports over the crunching of hungry mares.

A portable RCA was selected for his wife—a gift to liven up a housewife's routine. With enough batteries to operate for hours, it reverberated with plenty of volume and depth and could be toted from room to room or outside to the clothesline.

By the 1950s, televisions had killed the show for old-timey radios, and they began to fall out of fashion; but not for Early, who faithfully followed the stories—from the Pearl Harbor crisis to the latest "Amos and Andy" skit—on the radio. Radios, for him, had become indispensable. They had delivered the news that changed his life and the lives of his neighbors. They had brought words from leaders far and near. They had filled his home with music and unforgettable voices. And radios had brought his family together for hours at a time, filling the days with marvelous, electromagnetic inspiration.

WE INTERRUPT THIS BROADCAST

As you begin collecting radios, the following information may be helpful.

HISTORY OF THE RADIO

• In the 1800s, a British physicist, James Clerk Maxwell, hypothesized that it would one day be possible to send electromagnetic waves through space from electrical impulses. Several decades later, German scientist Heinrich Hertz proved that theory to be true. Using a machine called an oscillator, he experimented with transmitting Hertzian waves, now known as radio waves.

• By the late 1800s, a number of inventors were creating radio devices for detecting and sending radio waves.

• Radio was first used for transmitting signals to and from ships. Broadcasting to the public did not begin until 1920, when the results of the Harding-Cox presidential election were broadcast.

• By 1921, several radio stations had been established. Later that year, a telephone hookup connecting New York City and Chicago radio stations broadcast the Princeton-Chicago football game.

• There was a ban on manufacturing home radio sets during World War II.

GETTING STARTED COLLECTING

• Due to their availability and price, radios are easy to collect. Some sell for thousands of dollars but others can still be found for only a few dollars.

• Beware of reproductions, which can often be spotted by their perfect color intensity or flawless finish. If you find a "vintage" radio in "mint" condition, be wary and have it appraised. Radios were everyday appliances; they are rarely found unused.

• Collect by brand name, style, color, or era. Plastic tabletop radios in a variety of bright colors and Bakelite radios from the 40s, 50s, and 60s are currently prized collectibles.

• If a radio doesn't work, check inside the radio for a wiring diagram before paying to have it restored. Relatively simple technology may enable you to fix the set yourself if you can locate the necessary replacement parts.

A radio such as this can anchor a growing collection. Photo by Superstock.

• If you find a beautiful radio set that does not work and you are not technically inclined, at least make sure all the tubes are present. Otherwise, restoration may be quite costly.

RADIO MODELS

• Vintage radios included table and floor models fashioned from wood, metal, Catalin, Bakelite, and, later, plastic.

• Accompanying radio speakers range from basic horn types to cone-shaped, ornamental paper varieties with lavish designs.

• A "silent radio" was manufactured in 1938—a deco Bakelite radio that could be connected to a pillow speaker.

• Portability and low cost made transistor radios popular in the 1950s. Subcategories included micros, minis, and toy or boy radios.

• Novelty radios were fashioned into such shapes as books, phones, and cartoon characters and became ideal advertising and promotional tools.

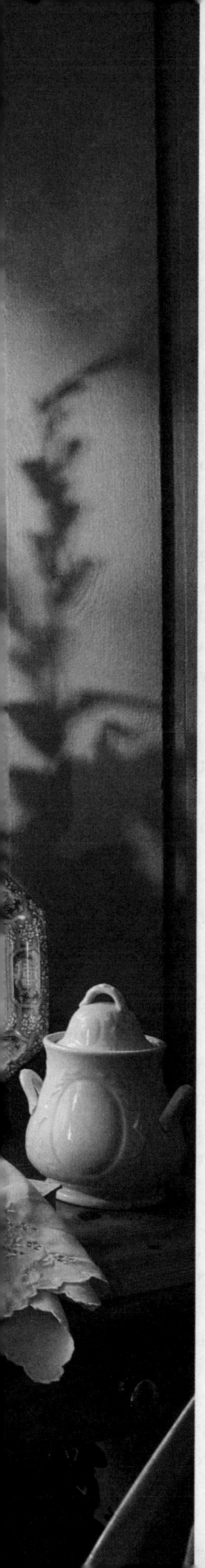

Message to a Dear Friend

Grace V. Watkins

I wish you quiet things:
Seagulls on upward wings
That seek the sunlit blue
And silver moonlight through
A wood when night is new.

I wish you joyful things:
Sweet cello murmurings
Of wind on golden hills
And dawn-bright daffodils
And little meadow rills.

I wish you holy things:
A gloried faith that sings,
An eagerness to share,
And every day a fair,
Love-lighted time of prayer.

To You

Louise Weibert Sutton

A pot of gold be yours today,
The gold of loving thought;
A treasure trove of gems be yours
From kindnesses well-wrought.
The beauty of content be yours,
With friendships tried and true,
And happy hours of fond recall
When this bright day is through.

If I could take the scarf of wind
And sequin it with stars,
If I could lift the stuff of dreams
That blend with soft guitars,

If I could reach into the air
And draw out, silken fine,
The gossamer of lovely hopes
To give life more of shine,

I'd box them up in tissues white
And ribbon them with smiles,
Then with the stamps of kind regard
I'd send them o'er the miles.
I'd put a card with them to say,
"Best wishes, fond and true,
From friend to friend, plus every joy!"
And mail them all to you.

A beautiful tablescape creates a place to think of friends. Photo by Jessie Walker.

LEGENDARY AMERICANS

Nancy Skarmeas

SAMUEL F. B. MORSE

Samuel Morse always knew he wanted to create something. As a young college student he believed that painting was the key to a creative life. Against the wishes of his parents, who imagined their son pursuing a more serious career, Morse graduated from Yale with dreams of being a famous artist. He traveled to England to further his training. After four years, Morse returned to the United States and settled in New York to begin his career as a painter.

Morse had wonderful visions of creating grand historical paintings; but such works required the support of patrons, and Morse could find none interested. He turned his considerable painting skills to portrait painting, which at least guaranteed an income, and also secured a teaching position in the art department at the University of the City of New York (later New York University).

Samuel Morse had carved out a creative life for himself, but it was not a life that made him happy. While struggling to make ends meet as an artist, Morse discovered he had another desire nearly as strong as his need to create. He wanted to be independently wealthy, and he was increasingly aware with the passing of each year that portrait painting would never satisfy that desire.

In 1832, Morse came upon an idea he believed would fulfill his need to create as well as his need for economic security. It was an idea that would transform Samuel Morse from painter into inventor and, eventually, transform the way Americans communicated across the country's expanding distances.

Samuel Morse, born in 1791 in Charleston, Massachusetts, was just over forty years old when his great moment of inspiration struck. He was crossing the Atlantic aboard the ship *Sully* after a trip through Europe studying painting. He was, at the time, still a portrait painter, still mildly unsatisfied with the course of his life. He was looking, actively or not, for something more to consume his energies. And he found that something more aboard that ship, through the serendipitous moment that he overhead a conversation about something called the electromagnet.

Morse had been fascinated with the idea of electricity since hearing a series of lectures on the subject at Yale. And aboard the *Sully*, in the middle of the vast waters of the Atlantic Ocean, that old interest and his current unsatisfied ambitions came together in the form of a wonderful idea. Morse disembarked after that crossing, determined to use the latest discoveries about electricity to create a machine that could send messages across wires stretched between cities and towns.

The idea of the telegraph was not entirely new. A Dutch scientist had done some preliminary work on a similar project a decade and a half earlier, and many others had tried to envision ways of using the newly discovered powers of electricity to communicate across distances. But Morse knew nothing of this. He was an artist with an interest in electricity, not a scientist. To him, the idea was a lightning bolt of inspiration, and he resolved to devote his life to the pursuit of this new invention. He began using his offices at New York University to build early models of the telegraph. Morse had little money to pour into his invention, so he used materials at hand, including an old clockworks and a homemade battery. By 1835, Morse had a working model of the telegraph operating in his office.

By 1837, Morse felt his work was progressing well enough to take on two partners, one with mechanical training and the resources of his family's iron works and another with the scientific expertise to improve the electrical components of the telegraph. But the driving force remained Samuel Morse, who grew more determined by the day to produce a workable telegraph.

Morse applied for his first patent on the telegraph in 1837. This primitive telegraph used a system where a dot and dash code represented numbers. Those numbers were then transformed into words with the use of a special dictionary created by Morse. Within a year, Morse had improved his code system, dropping the numbers and using a dot-dash code that directly translated to letters.

With his machine ready and his code perfected, Morse began to look for investors who shared his belief that the telegraph was a workable and potentially valuable invention. Private business was skeptical and hesitant to provide funding. As years passed, even Morse's partners began to lose hope. But Morse persevered, turning to Congress to find the money to build a telegraph line to test his invention. In 1843, the money was forthcoming; and within another year, a test line was complete, running from Washington, D.C., to Baltimore.

On May 24, 1844, came the moment Morse had worked for and dreamed about for twelve years. Morse tapped out his Morse code message, which traveled the forty-one-mile line in less than a minute. Morse selected a Biblical quote for this historic first telegraph, "What Hath God Wrought!" He chose this particular passage to express the wonder he felt at the marvel of electricity and his amazement that he had been the one to harness these marvels to create the telegraph.

Samuel Morse's need to create and his desire for financial success had finally found common ground. The success of the telegraph gave Morse the satisfac-

tion of creation as well as the promise of great financial rewards and gave Americans their first exhilarating taste of immediate communication between their cities and towns. The skeptical American people quickly reversed themselves and embraced the new invention as well as the inventor who had worked so single-mindedly to bring it about. In less than two years from that first test message, private companies were building telegraph lines at a furious pace and had already connected from Washington north to Boston and northwest to Buffalo. By 1861, the country was linked coast to coast by telegraph lines. The telegraph would be the front line of communication in America for the remainder of the nineteenth century. Samuel Morse had not only achieved a personal success, he had also transformed American life.

Samuel Morse himself became an American hero, a symbol of the American belief in innovation and ambition. In 1847, Morse realized one of his greatest dreams. With money earned from the telegraph, he bought a country estate for himself and his family near Poughkeepsie, New York. Morse lived another three decades, enjoying the admiration of the American people as well as the life of a wealthy philanthropist. He gave money to colleges and universities, to community charities, and, perhaps most significantly, to struggling artists, allowing them the freedom to create without financial worries.

Samuel Morse died in New York City in April of 1872. He was eighty years old. He is enshrined in the National Inventors Hall of Fame and remembered in every accounting of American history for his revolutionary innovation. As a young man, Samuel Morse knew that his life's calling was to be a creator. He thought he would create masterpieces on canvas. In the end, he could not have been disappointed. For although he exchanged brushes and paints for electricity and wire, Morse's greatest work, the telegraph, most certainly must be called a masterpiece of invention.

Nancy Skarmeas is a book editor and mother of two young children, who keep her and her husband quite busy at their home in New Hampshire. Her Greek and Irish ancestry has fostered a lifelong interest in research and history.

LOCUST GROVE, THE SAMUEL MORSE HISTORIC SITE
POUGHKEEPSIE, NEW YORK

Christine Landry

When I was young, I remember movies in which Morse code was used to save the day. I recall submarine scenes in which ambient tapping was ignored until an actor noticed a distinct rhythm to the sound. Recognizing it as Morse code, a scramble would follow to decipher the tapping and begin a rescue. However, I never really considered the origins of Morse code and the telegraph until a recent visit to Locust Grove, The Samuel Morse Historic Site in Poughkeepsie, New York, which surprisingly proved to be the house of an artist.

This National Historic Landmark was built in 1830 and was purchased by Samuel F. B. Morse in 1847. The money he acquired with the invention and success of the telegraph allowed him to buy the sizable property. Since then, Locust Grove has gone through many renovations. It was originally built in a Federal design; however, Morse employed his friend, the renowned architect Alexander Jackson Davis, to renovate it into the Tuscan building that can be viewed today. This transformation included a tower offering a panoramic view of property that comprises 150 acres. The land is dotted with locust trees and holds many gardens designed by Morse. Locust Grove also contains an extensive art collection, as Morse was both a painter and a collector.

Morse once expressed in a letter to his brother, "You have no idea how lovely Locust Grove is. Not a day goes by that I do not feel it." I too was surprised to see how lovely the property was. The main house, situated at the top of a bluff, is white and trimmed in blue-gray with arched windows. The design was inspired by Morse's art tour in Italy. Indeed, I felt as if I were visiting an Italian villa rather than a home in New York. A four-story, tower-like structure dominates one side of the building and can be viewed from many points in the surrounding landscape. Another Morse addition includes a three-story octagonal structure that juts to the side of the building. The lowest level is shaded by a veranda and is the perfect place to read or to contemplate the scenery.

Walking into the house, I was struck by its grandeur. An Oriental rug runs the length of the gleaming white front hall. Dark-wood furniture lines the hallway, and paintings adorn the walls. Located on the first floor of the tower, the drawing room displays Morse's desire to view and frame the outside world with windows as if it were a painting. Sheer curtains edge the large bay windows and allow the room to be washed in light. White and dark-wood furniture alternate within the setting to create an airy atmosphere of casual elegance.

The splendor of the surrounding land matched the splendor of the house. The walking trails guided me along the Geometric Garden, the Vegetable Garden, and the waterfall. Morse claimed the latter to be his favorite spot in Locust Grove; and after listening to the waterfall as it poured into a reflective pool, I can certainly understand why.

Before I left the scenic landscape of Locust Grove, I paid Morse Gallery a visit. There I was able to view a replica of the original telegraph; and in the Visitor Center, I was even able to practice Morse code. Although Morse's name will always be associated with his invention, Locust Grove reveals the soul of the artist that was also very much a part of Morse. In the lines of his house, the views from his windows, and the careful layout of his gardens, Morse fashioned Locust Grove as a place of beauty that can be appreciated by many visitors to come.

An archway frames an autumnal view of Locust Grove. Photo by Fred Otte, courtesy of Locust Grove, The Samuel Morse Historic Site.

There may be moments in
friendship, as in love,
when silence is beyond words.
—Ouida

Friends

Billy Cooper

They have communication which is not
Spoken aloud in words. On sunny days
They sit together on the bench outside
The feed store; but when air is raw and chill,
They go inside to chairs around the stove
And, still unspeaking, sit the long day through
In cozy silence. There's no need of talk
Between friends of long standing; years have wrought
A depth of clear perception and a warm
Association without spoken thought.
They greet each other amicably and nod
Goodbye when they are parting company.
Other than that respect of one another,
Neither breaks the silence of the other.

In this original painting by artist George Hinke, two longtime friends share a quiet game and a quiet day.

Old Letters

Adele Jordan Tarr

I keep your letters for a rainy day
Then take them out and read them all again.
So, reading, I forget that skies are gray
And pathways sodden under falling rain.

They are so full of simple friendliness,
Of understanding of the things I love.
No phrase obscure or vague to make me guess,
No deep philosophy my soul to move.

And though your eyes are "lifted to the hills,"

You still keep faith with earth and earthy things;
Prosaic duty all your hour fills
The while you listen for the beat of wings.

You have read deeply in the book of life,
And you have added lines that I shall keep
To be a shield against the petty strife,
Until such time as I shall fall asleep.

So when I would forget that skies are gray,
I read your letters on a rainy day.

Letters

Ruth B. Field

A few words drifting over time and space
Can bring warmth, a glow of friendliness;
A voice unheard, a loved one's absent face
Return with written words. A soft caress,
The echo of an old, forgotten song,
Between the lines, a sudden, clear reflection
To fill the heart with pleasure, deep and strong,
Brings back again a voice's dear inflection.
Across the miles, the handclasp of a friend
Reaches out within a letter's lines,

And down a little lane dream-footsteps wind
Where memory's flowered tendril greenly twines.
From old friends come small messages we love;
Just little things that bring a bit of cheer,
And, like sun smiling through the clouds above,
Are cherished words of someone we hold dear.
Oh, letters are like angels without wings
That come to us as if on magic flight,
Can evoke tears or happiness that sings,
Bright, little flames that light the darkest night.

Love is the life of friendship, letters are
The life of love, the loadstones that by rare
Attraction make souls meet and melt and mix,
As when by fire exalted gold we fix.
—A. Bronson Alcott

A young writer ponders her next line in THE LETTER *by artist Albert Lynch. Image from Christie's.*

HANDMADE HEIRLOOM

❖ ❖ ❖

Even novices can create beautiful marbleized designs such as this one. Photo by Superstock.

MARBLEIZED PAPER

Lisa Ragan

As a lifelong bibliophile, I love to frequent antique stores in search of old, leather-bound books to add to my collection. I do not, however, always select books based on the quality of the poetry or prose but rather fall in love with the feel of the rich, embossed leather in my hands and the beauty of the marbleized endpapers.

Upon returning home recently with a book that had particularly vivid endpapers, I began composing a letter to an old friend for whom I had purchased the book. I searched my desk for stationery to no avail when an idea occurred to me. Since I've always treasured the marbleized endpapers in old books, I resolved to make my own marbleized stationery.

Simply put, marbleized paper is achieved by floating paints or inks on water (or a thickened water solution), manipulating the colors into a desired pattern, then transferring that pattern onto paper. The earliest

record of this enchanting art form takes us to twelfth-century Japan, where artisans of the royal household created marbleized papers for calligraphy and poetry by using a process called *suminagashi*, which translates to "ink floating." After achieving a meditative state of inner and outer calm, these Japanese artisans floated Asian inks called sumi inks on water, blew or fanned the inks to create a pattern, and then captured that design by laying paper on top of the inks. The resulting marbleized papers were reserved for the sole use of Japanese nobility, and the process itself was kept secret for more than four hundred years.

A similar art form called *ebru*, a Turkish word meaning "cloud art," emerged in fifteenth-century Persia, India, and Turkey. In *ebru*, paints are floated atop thickened water and swirled into delicate patterns. The *ebru* method of marbleizing paper slowly spread to Europe by the sixteenth century and became popular in the endpapers of the bookbinding industry. In the tradition of Japanese nobility centuries before, European marblers also kept the process a guarded secret.

As the popularity of marbleized papers grew, English bookbinders began to import the papers from Holland and Germany. In order to avoid taxes, wily Dutch marblers wrapped the papers around toys before shipping them to England. The English bookbinders then ironed the resulting wrinkles in order to salvage the imported papers.

The demand for marbleized papers, particularly in books, grew steadily until it peaked during the late nineteenth century. By this time marbleized papers could be found on lampshades, wall hangings, and boxes as well as on books throughout Europe and the United States. The marbleizing process had remained a mystery to the general public until 1853 when English marbler Charles Woolnough published *The Art of Marbling* and revealed the process to the world. In 1885, the United States published a German book, *The Progress of the Marbling Art,* which explained the marbling process in simpler terms. But just as the marbling art fell into the hands of the common man, binding machines were invented and replaced hand binders and paper marblers.

Today, paper marbling has enjoyed a renaissance as interest in bookmaking, papermaking, and calligraphy has increased. Although modern-day crafters may experiment with various marbling formulas, a significant number still use methods and materials much like those used in Asia during the twelfth century.

To marbleize using a process similar to *suminagashi,* fill a tray about two-thirds full with tap water (at room temperature) and place it on a protected work surface in a well-ventilated area. Kitty litter pans (new or sterilized), aluminum foil roasting pans, or photo trays work well for marbling trays. The marbling tray should be larger than the paper by about an inch on all sides.

Choose colors in artist's oils or drawing inks. To mix and test colors, assemble a collection of watercolor trays, ice cube trays, or baby food jars. If using oil paint, thin each color with turpentine. Wearing latex gloves, experiment with each color by placing a drop of color on the surface of the water to see how it will respond. Depending on the type of paint used, each color may react differently on the water and may require a different combination of paint and turpentine. Ideally, the drop of color should spread a few inches in diameter, maintain its hue, and remain on top of the water.

Once the colors have been mixed and tested, clean any dust or residual color off the water by skimming the water with strips of newspaper. Then gently add drops of color to the water one by one with an eyedropper or several drops at once with a broomcorn whisk brush. Using any of a variety of tools, such as a toothpick, straight pin, or even a cat's whisker, gingerly swirl the colors together into a design. Marbleized papers provide a one-time snapshot of a design in constant flux; no design can ever be truly replicated. Marblers must relinquish the need for total control over the finished design and instead work *with* the colors, which will move and change of their own accord.

Have absorbent paper close by. When a pleasing design appears, grasp a piece of absorbent paper by the opposite corners and roll carefully onto the water. Make sure the entire surface of the paper is touching the marbling mixture. Let the paper stand for one or two seconds and then carefully remove from the tray. Regular typing paper that has a high cotton content works well, as does rice paper, construction paper, and even coffee filters. Hang the marbleized paper to dry or lay flat on newspaper. Like the English bookbinders of yesteryear, present-day marblers can remove wrinkles by ironing the wrong side of the dried paper.

Marblers may attempt to copy some of the classic designs, such as French curl (also called snail), Italian vein pattern, Turkish stone, and Spanish wave. Other traditional patterns include peacock (also called bouquet), nonpareil, zebra, curtain, and feather.

As for my marbleized stationery, I was pleased with the results that even a novice like me can accomplish. Although I don't think I quite achieved a meditative state of inner and outer calm like the Japanese artisans centuries ago, I did enjoy both the process and the final results. What a joy to discover this ancient art form that has come to us from both Eastern and Western civilizations. And best of all, what was once a guarded secret, passed down through the generations, has now become an heirloom art form available to everyone.

Friendship

Sudie Stuart Hager

Friendship is a common home-grown flower,
But most uncommon are its growing ways.
Its seed can quicken, root within an hour;
Its lovely bloom survive the wintriest days.
It bears transplanting best when fully grown
With roots fine-tendriled, spreading wide and deep;
Removed, it lives on memory-soil alone—
A phantom field where death-winds ever sweep.
It is refreshed by fountains long gone dry,
This everlasting flower that will not die.

Seeds of Friendship

Helen Virden

He never knew the miracles he wrought
In lives of neighbors that he named as friend;
The simple deeds of kindness that he taught
In lessons that "heart-tenants" comprehend.
He knew an honesty as strong as steel,
Integrity that sorted right from wrong.
He owned a humble spirit that could kneel
To praise his God and pass his faith along.

He lit small fires of friendship where he walked,
For he was quick with laughter or a joke.
Unselfishness would echo when he talked;
Warm loyalty would edge each word he spoke.

He sowed the world with friendship, kindly deeds,
And goodness blossoms daily from those seeds.

Bouquets tempt visitors to the farmer's market in San Luis Obispo, California. Photo by Londie G. Padelsky.

The Distant View

Fleta Pierce Newlin

Sometimes the days are long without a sight
Of your dear smile; I yearn to see your face
And hear your voice exchanging commonplace
Remarks with mine. Nor does a day take flight
From us wherein I think not with delight
Of you, my friend; for neither absence, space,
Nor time can dull the wonder and the grace
Of friendship's sweet communion, ever bright.

I know that I can see, away from you
(As climbers see more clearly from the plain
The grand, majestic beauty of the wane
And rise of peaks beyond, through distant view),
The love and strength and courage of your heart;
Thus we renew our friendship when apart.

When you part from your friend, you grieve not, for that

which you love most in him may be clearer in his absence, as the

mountain to the climber is clearer from the plain.—Kahlil Gibran

*The sunset lights a hillside covered with bunchgrass, paintbrush, and balsam root
in Oregon's Zumwalt Prairie Preserve. Photo by Mary Liz Austin.*

Prayer

Helen Williams

I ask not for Your gifts to bring
To me undying fame,
Nor wish to see in blazoned lights
The letters of my name.
I ask You not for might and power;
I ask not costly dress,
Nor pray for gold that others seek
Their lives and ways to bless.
I would not have the strength and wealth
That glorifies a king;
And yet, O Lord, I humbly kneel
And ask for but one thing:
I only pray as down life's path
My way I slowly wend,
Almighty Father, teach me how
To be a loyal friend.

The Fairest Gift

Lillian Terhune

If I should place a value on
The bounty of the earth,
Which would I say, of all its joys,
Has quite the greatest worth?

Would I name education, gold,
Or fame that fortune lends?
No, this I think is best of all—
The priceless gift called friends.

A lakeside blanket offers a delightful spot for tea.
Photo by ImageState.

Devotions FROM THE Heart

Pamela Kennedy

"Henceforth I call you not servants; for the servant knoweth not what his lord doeth: but I have called you friends; for all things that I have heard of my Father I have made known unto you. Ye have not chosen me, but I have chosen you." John 15:15–16a

CHOOSING TO HAVE FRIENDS

The teenaged girl rushed into my classroom early, slid into her desk, and dropped her backpack on the floor with a thud. Her round, dimpled face softened into a smile as she saw me.

"Good morning, Mrs. Kennedy. I'm hoping you are having a good day?"

"Yes, Oksana. It's a beautiful morning, isn't it? How are you?"

"Oh, I am so in a hurry. I am trying to study for chemistry exam. I think I am losing it or whatever." She plunged both arms into the backpack, digging through notebooks, spilling pencils and pens. "Ah, here it is!" She triumphantly waved a paper folder above her head. "I am not lost after all!"

"Oksana, how are you doing besides chemistry?" I asked. "Are you very lonely?" The girl was an exchange student spending a year in Hawaii, thousands of miles from her home in Azerbaijan.

"Some days it is hard. But now I have some friends. That is better. Before, when I first come, it is as though no one needs a new friend. Everyone has enough already. Then it was much more lonely."

We talked for a few minutes about her home and her plans for college when she returned to her native country. Then she was off to see the chemistry teacher. But her words haunted me the rest of the day. "No one needs a new friend. Everyone has enough already." In those simple phrases, this teenager had exposed the two sides of loneliness. And I realized it is not only about lacking friends but also about making room to accept new friends.

It is easy enough for me to recall the times when I felt lonely because I needed a friend. After twenty-eight years of moving around with the military, I was an expert on that subject. But Oksana made me consider something else. How many times had I imposed loneliness upon someone else because I had decided I didn't need any new friends? Had I ever considered that what I really needed was to reach out and to lessen the loneliness of another?

In the passage from John above, Jesus is speaking to His disciples. He has just told them they need to stay close to Him, to abide in Him and to obey Him, but then He speaks these tender words: "I have called you friends . . . I have chosen you." How comforting it must have been for the followers of Christ to hear this affirmation. Many had left family and home to follow Jesus. They were identifying with a controversial character and experiencing rejection from many of their peers. They needed someone to reach out and make room for friendship. And Jesus did. He announced that He was going to let them in on the most intimate details of His life. He was opening His heart to them by choice; and in doing so, He was flooding their loneliness with His love.

What a model for us. We too are surrounded by people who are lonely and are convinced no one cares to make time for them. Our challenge is to decide how to respond. We can determine that we already have enough friends. Or we can choose to follow the example of Christ by enlarging our boundaries and welcoming new friends into our lives. And, if we choose the latter, in the end we may just discover that we need them even more than they need us!

Dear Jesus, help me to follow You by willingly opening my heart to extend and accept friendship.

Friends share the chore of gathering a bouquet in PICKING FLOWERS by Winslow Homer. Image from Christie's.

Loaf with Me

Leonard G. Nattkemper

Oh, come with me, my friend,
And loaf a little while.
A day or two we'll spend
In good old-fashioned style.

We'll cut across the town
To find a trail I know
And watch it wind around
To where wildflowers grow.

We'll take a little snack
Of good, old, common fare
And tie our kit and pack
Upon us anywhere.

We'll leave the city's roar
And all our cares behind
And tramp a mile or more
Upon the trail we find.

We'll have the open sky
To keep us company
Where singing birds wing by
In sweetest harmony.

We'll smell from flowers in bloom
And from the scented grass,
Old-fashioned sweet perfume
Along the streams we pass.

We'll take a thumb-eared book,
The kind we love the best,
And sit beside a brook
And read and yawn and rest.

And when the shades of night
Have closed upon the day,
We'll sleep beneath the starlight
And dream the night away.

Friends find a place to loaf in GIRLS WITH A WREATH OF FLOWERS *by
William Brymner. Image from Superstock.*

FOR THE CHILDREN

My Puppy Learned to Read Today

Ruth Townsend

My puppy learned to read today,
And this is how I know:
I put his name there on his house
And printed it just so.

He used to let the cats go in,
And he would stay outside;
But with his name all printed there,
He looks at it with pride.

He's in there now as pleased as punch.
He'll never start to roam.
He's found a place that's really his.
It's not a house, it's home!

Champ gets a home of his own in PUPPY'S PALACE,
an original oil painting by artist Donald Zolan.

Where Did Summer Go?

William Arnette Wofford

Where did the bright-winged summer go?
Ah, is there any who can say?
She surely vanished overnight,
For the goldenrod's in bloom today.

It seems but yesterday that June
Came in the door on dancing feet.
The roses flamed; the sky was blue,
The honeysuckle, white and sweet.

The sunny days stretched endlessly,
And mountains lured with cooling shade;
The distant seaside's mighty waves
Beckoned where happy children played.

But now, where has the summer gone?
I've searched for her but all in vain.
Can it be true September's here,
The first leaf fallen in the lane?

The meadow wind cannot tell me,
Nor does the busy squirrel know;
Yet still my heart has but one cry:
Oh, where, oh, where did summer go?

Aster and goldenrod forecast the changing season near La Grange, Kentucky. Photo by Daniel Dempster.

Good books, like friends,
    are things we treasure:
Both sources of unending pleasure,
Both can inspire, both entertain,
Both worth far more than worldly gain.
    —Isla Paschal Richardson

Downtown Library

Violet L. Gregory

I feel the need of books!
In my city I go to the square
In the heart of its busiest section
Where, set like a gem in a cast-iron setting,
Is a low and gracious white stone building.
From the rush and glare of the streets
Through a wide glass-paneled door
I walk, and a sanctuary
Of stillness takes me in.
There is balm in the quiet aisles
To sooth pinpoints of care,
And a benediction falls
To fill any waiting cup.
Yet there to my hand and eye
Are rows and rows of books,
The minted treasures, culled from time,
To be newly mined by me today.
Then I tuck them under my arm
And carry their beauty home.

Walled by a Book

Elinor Lennen

Walled by a book, however fierce the storm,
One need not hear the wind nor feel the cold.
Words build a shelter, adequate and warm,
Which years cannot attack nor use make old.
How many others, on what other days,
Sought this retreat and claimed it for a time,
Protected from life's hazards by a phrase,
Companioned by a story or a rhyme?

Men yet unborn shall seek this tried defense
When refuge fails that seemed secure and strong,
Shall balance losses by the recompense
Of sober truth, of stirring tale or song.
Give him no sorry sigh nor pitying look
Who has the single solace of a book!

I count good books among my better friends,
The wisdom of the ages they unfold;
I share the thoughts of sages of the past
And feel I have unearthed a vein of gold.
    —Harold G. Hopper

The library table holds a collection of classics in A Book of Poems by artist Claude Raguet Hirst. Image from Christie's.

POEMS
UPON
SEVERAL OCASIONS

THE CHOICE
LOVE TRIUMPANT
AND OWD RUSSO
EPISTLES
CRUELTY AND LUST

ON THE DIVINE ATTR
IBUTES
A PROSPECT OF DEATH
ON THE CONFLAGRAT
ON AND LAST JUDGMEN

BY THE
REV JOHN POMFRET
WITH THE
LIFE OF THE AUTHOR
LONDON
PRINTED FOR W. SUTTABY
COURT
1808

My Teacher

Alexander Wiley

She was no purveyor of mere facts.
With her, grades were not the thing.
She had enthusiasm—
    the Greek's "fire of the soul."
And she gave of it, and giving,
Her students caught the flame.
Building men was her task.
She told us to dream dreams,
Build ourselves a great plan of life,
Full of joy and vision.

With her nothing was
    dull and monotonous.
Every bit of learning
    was a step to nobler truth.
Life was a mysterious adventure.
We were growing units of a perfect entity.
We were singers of a great symphony.
We were seekers for more light.
Glad and joyous was she,
And she taught us to be likewise.

A teacher greets her returning children in BACK TO SCHOOL by Henry Jules Jean Geoffroy. Image from Christie's Images/Superstock.

No task was drudgery,
    but an opportunity for growth.
In helping others,
    we helped ourselves, she said.
We were like Millet—
Painting pictures for eternity.
We were called to great things.
She fed us self-reliance
    and the dignity of life;
She taught us to think,
    to breathe, to feel life!

To get rid of fear and ignorance
And dare to go out and do.
Radiant was this woman.
Like sunshine was her presence,
And her influence was like the dawn.
You speak of money and things,
You who find life but a grabbing process.
Learn of her as we have learned,
And you will find a new meaning
To this link in the chain we call life.

Lines to an Old Schoolhouse

Priscilla Jane Thompson

Dear school of my childhood,
      thrice dear doth thou seem,
Now that thou shalt soon be no more;
Oh, fresh in my memory, sweet visions gleam,
Reflecting the bright days of yore.
Those days when we played with our faces abeam,
And manhood and womanhood seemed but a dream.
Thy grove, cool and shady, with maples o'ergrown,
Has sheltered us all in the past;
We've romped 'neath thy shadows
    while bright years have flown,
Too sweet and too pleasant to last.
Dear school of my childhood, with pain in my heart,
I yield to grim progress and see thee depart.
And all of our teachers: how bright in our mind,
We recall every one as they came;
Each, like a wise monarch, unselfish and kind,
Did make our advancement their aim.
Think not that the scholar ne'er valued thy care;
Thy teachings sank deeper than thou wert aware.
Thy dear grove has sheltered, when life seemed a care,
And trials have clouded our way.
And oft the young lover and sweet maiden fair
Have wooed here where once they did play.
Oh, fresh in our memories e'er wilt thou be,
Since the skein of our childhood is woven with thee!
Dear Amity, emblem of friendship's pure gold,
We shall not bemoan thee, as past.
E'en now, like that fabulous phoenix of old,
From thy ashes, a new school looms vast.
More comely in structure, we view it nearby
And hail thy successor with pride in our eye.
We dread not the future, oh, Amity new.
What else canst thou do but succeed;
Thy ancestor's mantle has fallen to you,
    And we know thou'lt supply ev'ry need.
    May thy present scholars, and those to enroll,
    Inscribe a good record upon thy fair scroll.

Golden maples shade a schoolyard near Hamburg, Wisconsin. Photo by Ken Dequaine.

September

Kay Hoffman

September is betwixt-between
Autumn's gold and summer's green,
Not still quite summer, yet not fall,
But cool enough to wear a shawl.

Songbirds have left for southern clime
But some still think it's summertime
And linger, when the others fly,
To let us know they're standing by.

The leaves aquiver on the tree
Seem unsure of what their role will be.
While some are edged with autumn's gold,
Others to summer's green still hold.

The rose clings to her summer pride
And blushes like a sweet June bride;
When comes the purple shades of night,
Gold harvest moon steals her delight.

We greet thee autumn with warm "hello"
But hate to see the summer go.
September, you're one of our kind;
Like us, you can't make up your mind.

Branches form a quilt of color in Montreal's Mount Royal Park.
Photo by Superstock.

Raven Creek

Dean Robbins

Let's stop to watch the leaves
Fall into Raven Creek
And start their journey to
Whatever dead leaves seek.

The dawn has left its dew
To drench the grass. We'll stand,
For water's still as wet
When glistening on land.

We'll skip a stone across
To where it might have been
And then some other day,
We'll skip it back again.

We'll stay for just a while;
The leaves will fall all day.
But when the morning's gone,
We'd best be on our way.

And then we'll walk back home,
Content with our first peek
At autumn as the leaves
Fall into Raven Creek.

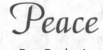

Peace

Bee Bacherig

This is the very spot for me—
A big root 'neath a giant oak tree.
I'll sit and watch the creek below
And now and then a pebble throw.
I'll just forget the book I brought,
For here I've found the peace I sought.

Autumn abounds in things to

delight the senses and the spirit.

—Esther York Burkholder

*Red maple leaves cover a streambed in Wyman Township, Maine.
Photo by William H. Johnson.*

September

Elzora Duncan

If I were September,
I would give you
A day far from the city,
A walk through an autumn wood,
A cool brook to dangle your feet in,
An afternoon sun to warm your back,
A collage of red and gold leaves
    on a distant hillside,
The sounds of twilight,
Lowing of cattle, quail calling,
Farm dogs barking,
The early hoot of an owl.
A new awareness, peace
    with yourself.
These things I would give you—
If I were September.

September Afternoon in the Woods

Grace V. Watkins

Today the trees are violins
Where brown and golden music sings
As small, adventuring breezes draw
Their gentle bows across the strings.
And in my heart a song and prayer
Are shining and September fair.

*A golden branch crosses a cluster of aspens in
Colorado's West Elk Wilderness. Photo by Carr Clifton.*

AUTUMN STILLNESS

Naomi I. Parks

Silently, in stealth and beauty,
Brilliant color claims the land
Through the lowlands, o'er the mountains,
Scarlet, golden drifting bands.
Touching all the leafy foliage,
Burning bright with smokeless flame,
Laughing at the wind and weather,
All the things that seek to tame.

Summer's days are slowly ending,
Soon they'll pass along the way,
Gone to join the countless sons
In the land of yesterday.
Lest our hearts be sad and grieving,
Autumn sounds the glorious call,
Borne upon the drifting breezes,
Reaching out to compass all.

Silently, in wordless wonder,
We behold the mystic change.
Unseen runners pass their torches,
Unrestricted in their range.
Shadows lengthen o'er the waters,
Forming bands of dark and light;
Autumn stillness seems to whisper,
"After me, comes winter's nights."

A small brook meanders through a maple forest near Lac La Belle in Michigan's Upper Peninsula. Photo by Ken Dequaine.

Readers' Forum

Snapshots from Our Ideals Readers

Top left: While vacationing in Hawaii, two-year-old Jacqueline Miller and her two-month-old brother, Max, find a palm tree that's just their size. Jacqueline and Max are the great-niece and -nephew of Dagmar L. Tonkovich of Downey, California.

Top right: Grandmother Sara N. Johnston of Greenbelt, Maryland, loves this photo of her favorite little ones, Nathaniel and Jewel Stafford, ages two-and-a-half-years and thirteen months.

Lower left: Samantha Browne is ready to teach her tiny cousin, Madison Mosley, all about the outside world. The girls' picture was sent to *Ideals* by their proud great-grandmother, Annabelle Lindley of Pasadena, Texas.

Top left: New big brother Robert Strehle, age two, discovers that caring for his five-week-old brother, Joshua, takes a lot of patience. The boys' grandmother, Donna H. Rice of Burton, Michigan, shared this endearing shot with us.

Top right: Elizabeth McIninch of Norcross, Georgia, shares this photo of her great-granddaughters. Two-and-a-half-year-old Jessica is all smiles while posing with her brand-new baby sister, Lauren.

Lower right: Three-year-old Jessica Kaye Seehafer stretches out for a photo with her new baby sister, Jennifer Ruth. The photograph was shared with us by the girls' great-grandmother, Sabilla Denholm of Webster, South Dakota.

THANK YOU Dagmar L. Tonkovich, Sara N. Johnston, Annabelle Lindley, Donna H. Rice, Elizabeth McIninch, Sabilla Denholm, Muriel Neeley, Marcia Hancock, and Sara Beddow for sharing your family photographs with *Ideals*. We hope to hear from other readers who would like to share snapshots with the *Ideals* family. Please include a self-addressed, stamped envelope if you would like the photos returned. Keep your original photographs for safekeeping and send duplicate photos along with your name, address, and telephone number to:

Readers' Forum
Ideals Publications
535 Metroplex Drive, Suite 250
Nashville, Tennessee 37211

Above: Muriel Neeley of Bellevue, Washington, shares this snapshot of her great-granddaughter, Nora Carter. Nora was very serious about enjoying her first birthday cake.

Below left: Landon Curry isn't quite sure if he is ready to turn two. The birthday boy's photo was sent to us by his grandmother, Marcia Hancock of Shoreline, Washington.

Below right: After enjoying a messy slice of birthday cake, three-year-old Christopher Blair of Naperville, Illinois, readjusts his party hat. This photo was taken by Christopher's great-aunt, Sara Beddow of Colorado Springs, Colorado.

ideals

Publisher, Patricia A. Pingry
Editor, Michelle Prater Burke
Managing Editor, Peggy Schaefer
Designer, Marisa Calvin
Production Manager, Travis Rader
Editorial Assistant, Patsy Jay
Contributing Editors, Lansing Christman, Pamela Kennedy, Nancy Skarmeas, and Lisa Ragan

ACKNOWLEDGMENTS

BENNETT, GERTRUDE RYDER. "Fisherman's Daughter" from *The Harvesters.* Copyright © 1967 by Golden Quill Press. Used by permission of Golden Quill Press, Tucson, AZ. CHAPPELL, ETHEL. "Summer Insured." Used by permission of Lisa H. Haner. FIELD, RUTH B. "Letters." Used by permission of Natalie Field Bevis. HOLMES, MARJORIE. "Summer Garden" from *You and I and Yesterday.* Reprinted by permission. Our sincere thanks to the following authors whom we were unable to locate: Billy Cooper for "Friends"; Will Evans for "Neighbors"; Sudie Stuart Hagar for "Friendship"; Edwin Markham for "We Have Broken Our Bread Together"; The Louise Moss Montgomery Estate for "Passing"; Florence Steigerwalt for "In Tune"; Adele J. Tarr for "Old Letters"; Lillian Terhune for "The Fairest Gift"; Alexander Wiley for "My Teacher."